# Sub Notes

## THE COMPLETE GUIDE to

## SUBSTITUTE TEACHING

Bob Peterson

DEDICATION

This book is dedicated to the students who deserve continuity and consistency of their school day even when the teacher is not present.

# CONTENTS

# ACKNOWLEDGMENTS

Thanks to all the secretaries, admins and staff that insure that the classrooms have a substitute teacher when necessary. The information you provide us first thing in the morning help define how effective we will be in the classroom.

Also, thanks to Gary, Phyllis and Marisa for your help reviewing this book.

# 1 Introduction

The information in this pamphlet is derived from my experiences as a substitute teacher over the last 3 $\frac{1}{2}$ years in both the public and charter schools in Florida. I have been a substitute in the elementary, middle, and high school settings. My preference is for middle school and high school. The purpose of this booklet is to add to the knowledge base of substitute teachers. I hope that it will better prepare you to cope with the challenges of the job.

The role of the substitute teacher is to provide consistency and continuity to the teacher's lesson plan and to maintain classroom discipline. Students do not like change. They respond positively to the routine that the teacher in a particular class maintains. This book is an attempt to help substitute teachers maintain that continuity of the lesson plan and classroom behavior as much as possible. Seems pretty simple. Like all plans they look good until you hit the battlefield then they may not be so good. More about that later.

My experience is that the teachers genuinely value the substitute teachers and understand our challenges. Many teachers have been substitute teachers and understand our challenges. They will be as helpful as they can be. The teachers in the classrooms near my classroom have always provided information, guidance, and support if asked. I've found, there is usually a team leader that you can go to for guidance.

## 2 Why be a Sub?

In my case (I am retired) it gives me both the opportunity to earn some extra money and the flexibility to control my schedule. I am an independent contractor so if I want to sub on a particular day, good, if not, good. Please note that the pay is marginal, generally in the $10/$13 per hour range. Sometimes it's the hardest $13.00 per hour I've ever earned; sometimes I get a lot of reading done. It provides me the opportunity to keep in touch with young people and observe up close and personal what they are thinking and doing. Additionally, it gives me an opportunity to see how my tax dollars are being spent.

Other reasons might be that you are a recent graduate who has not been hired by a school system. In Florida, there are over 10,000 (that's right over 10 thousand) applications waiting to be approved. (This issue is allegedly being resolved.) It gives you real-world experiences of what a teacher's day is like. It is like a paid internship but instead of being given all the menial jobs that have nothing to do with the job you are seeking; you are in a classroom with real students following the teacher's lesson plan. Bonus, you don't have to make coffee for the boss. It also could be a foot in the door at a particular school. Teachers leave all the time and replacements are needed. Maybe you were a stay at home Mom/Dad and your kids are now off to school and you're looking to pick up a little cash and get out of the house. Again, the money is not great but the flexibility can't be beaten.

## 3 Becoming a Substitute Teacher

My experience is in the state of Florida, but I think these requirements are consistent throughout the country.

1) You need at least 60 college credits and preferably a college degree.
2) You will need to pass a drug test
3) You must submit to a local/state criminal background check. In Florida, there is a cost to this, (about $80.00), and that is your responsibility. Each school district may require a background check and fingerprint at approx. $80.00 per district.
4) Upon successful completion of the background check and drug test, you will be issued a picture

ID. (I always wear mine so the kids can see it. It provides an air of officialdom.)

5) The final pre-employment hurdle is you may be required to take an online 20-hour Substitute Teaching course. Upon completion of the course material and quizzes, you will receive a certificate that you will send to the district. This certificate is good for five years and valid in any district in the state.

6) Once your application is accepted you will be instructed as to when and where orientation will be provided. Attendance is required before being allowed to step into a classroom.

# 4 **Orientation**

The substitute teacher orientation will consist of an overview of the district's policies, legal requirements, and expectations. Our orientation included a talk by a substitute liaison about demeanor and dress as well. A deputy from the sheriff's department talked about topics such as what to do if a fight breaks out, what to do in the classroom if there is an active shooter, and, how to handle unruly students, etc. **Pay attention.** During our presentation, we were shown weapons and drugs that had been confiscated the previous year. The talk about girls fighting was also an eye-opener. I will touch on this later but girls fight differently than boys. Generally speaking boys will stop fighting when an authority figure steps in and separates them. Girls will not. They will not separate and may even take a break and continue if allowed to. This orientation does not scratch the surface of what you will be experiencing but it is nonetheless good information.

# 5 Your Demeanor

A couple of quick notes about demeanor. Your job is to provide continuity and consistency to the teacher's lesson plan and maintain classroom order. You are not there to change anyone's life, to make friends with anyone, or to influence the students. This is not to say that anyone of those could not happen and if one was to positively influence a student it would be great but it is not your goal. You are there for a limited duration. To do your job you must be a professional. That means maintaining your composure, being **accepting** of all students, not copping an attitude, remaining responsive and receptive to each student. Honesty is huge. Be as frank as you can with the kids taking into account their feelings. (Unless their behavior warrants a reality check). It's a given that there are those kids that will attempt to push your buttons and try to manipulate you. You should know and expect this going in so it should not be a surprise. Do not lose your temper. It should never get that far. If that happens the student who pushed your buttons has won.

# 6 Getting a Sub Job

You are a private contractor. As such it is your responsibility to find work. The good news is there are a ton of schools and they all need substitute teachers. In Florida, once you have your ID it is accepted by any school in the (county-wide) district. The bad news is that if you want to sub in another district you have to go through the same process including paying for another background check and drug test. I also sub in a charter school. The requirements were not as stringent. They required a college degree, background check, and drug test but they accepted the county's background check and drug test since I had already passed them. That process moved much more quickly.

The public-school system has an "absence management" software application that I have access to. This program enables me to see what teachers will be absent on what days at which schools. As the teachers call out, their days are posted. Within the program, you can select what schools you want to work at. I have chosen to only be notified of positions in two schools: a high school and a middle school. These two schools are within ten minutes driving time so I am not going to burn a lot of time and gas going to and from $12.00 per hour job.

The charter school does not have access to this portal. You must get on the substitute teachers list that the school compiles. When a teacher wants to take off, they will call subs from the list. This is where you need to do some marketing. Essentially you are competing against the other subs on the list for a limited number of jobs. It will behoove you to get to know the teachers at the school and make sure they have your contact information so that they call/text/email you directly when they are sick or need to take off. This is where leaving the teacher good notes becomes important. The more feedback you give the teacher, the more likely they will want you over the other available options.

# 7 Starting the day

Generally, there is a designated person or two that you go to for the attendance roster, room key, and any other needed materials. This is your chance to ask questions to orientate yourself. Is this a normal schedule or is there some event you should be aware of and how will that affect the class schedule? Generally, the substitute liaison will tell you but it doesn't hurt to ask. Sometimes there are last-minute changes that they may have just heard about and forget to pass the information on. If you are not sure, ask what are the policies regarding removing a student or who should you call if there is an emergency. Ask for a copy of the phone extension list if you don't have one. If there are reward systems in use, such as Cane Cash request some. Cane Cash is a positive reward system utilizing paper money-like slips that the students can use within the school to purchase or rent supplies in the classroom. For example, if the student does not have a pencil they can rent one or buy one from the teacher using Cane Cash. It's purpose is to reward good behavior and teach personal responsibility. If special behavior referral forms are used, ask for a couple. Ask where you should go during lunch. Is there a refrigerator and microwave available? Is the room locked or is a code need?

# 8 Lesson Plan

The teacher will always provide a lesson plan. **REVIEW THE LESSON PLAN THOROUGHLY BEFORE THE STUDENTS ARRIVE.**

Some lesson plans are simply a post-it note with a pile of worksheets/handouts. Some are detailed lists of work to be completed, how the teacher wants it completed and when it is due. The teacher might also note which students will be helpful, who to keep an eye on, potential medical issues, and who the team leader is if help/guidance is necessary. Some teachers, particularly at the high school level will post the assignments on their website. If there are questions, ask another teacher/team leader for assistance before the kids get there.

My biggest concern (ok, fear) is that the lesson plan does not have enough work to keep the majority of the students busy for the entire period. By the way, this is also a teacher's biggest concern. They don't want to get to the end of their prepared lesson plan with time remaining. A teacher has the advantage of back-filling, the substitute does not. **Note to teachers**: please assign way more work than the students can complete. A class full of students with no work is a formula for bad things to happen. The sub can tell students who are concerned that they did not finish, "do the best you can, the teacher will know". It's not a bad idea to have a Quizlet (English and vocabulary) or a Kahn Academy account for math in your back pocket.

Students will ask if this work will be graded. I tell them it will count as a classwork grade. If they think this is busy work they won't do it and goof off all period (not good).

## 9 Classroom Norms

One of the main responsibilities of the substitute teacher is to maintain continuity of the environment as well as the lesson plan. The teacher will have trained the students in their classroom as to the acceptable norms of behavior. It is important to get a sense of what these norms are and attempt to maintain them as much as possible. This may include seating charts and whether the students are allowed to collaborate while doing their work. Some teachers allow the students to turn their desks to form small groups. There will be rules for going to the bathroom. Sometimes only one boy or one girl is allowed out at a time. Sometimes one of each is permitted to go at the same time. Generally, there is some type of bathroom pass or key and a sign-in/sign-out log. Some teachers allow students to listen to music on their phones and some require that the phones be turned off and put away. Sometimes the teacher is very precise about what their classroom norms and expectations are and sometimes they are not. The sub can generally get a sense of what the norms are by observing the setup of the classroom. Are the desks in neat rows, are there tables with several chairs around them, are the chairs stacked when you enter the classroom in the morning? Are there signs or posters on the walls indicating "NO PHONES or ELECTRONIC DEVICES"? That's a clue. Are there posters indicating "Voice Level "0" or "1""? (The schools that I sub at have a voice level system. 0= no talking, 1-4 =graduated levels of volume).

There will be a couple of students in every class that will try to manipulate the rules or norms. Whatever the psychological reason for this is, try not to fall for it. When you announce the assignment, they will tell you, "we've already done that". When you tell them to be quiet, they will tell you the teacher lets them talk or listen to music or get up and move around. If you ask the other students if this is so, generally the other students will support or at least not contradict the student's assertions. Sometimes the teacher will tell you which students will provide reliable information. Be careful how you ask them. You don't want to single them and subject them to trouble later. The better sense you have of the teacher's classroom standards the better off you will be in maintaining order. Remember, the majority of the students in the class want the classroom structure maintained. It's generally only a few that wants to destabilize the classroom norms.

## 10 **Pre class preparations**

When I get to the classroom in the morning, I write my name on the whiteboard. Next, I locate the "call button". Not that I want or intend to use it but I don't want to be searching for it if a kid has crossed the line to the extent that they need to be removed from class. There is generally a Substitute Folder with school information such as fire exits, the procedure for calling administration and school schedule. There also may be IEPs for some of the students. These are Individualized Educational Plans and may have good information. We go into educational plans in greater detail later in this pamphlet. They may tell you that Johnny should sit in front of the class or that JaShawn should not sit near Emily. They may tell you who gets additional time to complete an assignment. They also may tell you who has a **medical condition**. Good to know if someone has a kidney issue and needs to go to the bathroom every half hour or that someone is allergic to a perfume or peanut butter. Take note of this information.

Take a look around the room for clues regarding classroom norms. If there is a video projector/sound system that will be used during the class figure out how to use it before the students get there. At the beginning of each class, I stand at the entrance to the classroom and greet the students. I try to greet them by name. The problem comes when you greet one student by their name and the next student says, "do you remember my name?" and I don't. In that case, I tell them I don't remember, apologize and try to remember for the next time. I explain that I may have seen hundreds of students since I last saw them. That puts it in perspective for them.

## 11 Class time

During attendance I ask the students to be quiet, say "here" and raise their hand when I call their name. Most of the students will sit quietly during attendance but some will ignore you and continue to talk. This will be your first opportunity to identify students that may cause issues during the period. I also apologize in advance for mispronouncing their names and ask for corrections. Some of them I never get right. There can be two students with the same name, spelled the same and they want them pronounced differently. Who gets which pronunciation? Generally, it's the students that are disruptive whose name I remember.

If there are written notes or plans, I write them on the whiteboard if the teacher has not already done that. I read the teacher's plans to the students at the beginning of class and I also reference the whiteboard when reading the directions so the students know that the instructions are posted on the whiteboard. The instructions frequently need to be repeated multiple times throughout each class. This is normal. The students will frequently tell me that they have already done that work. My response is to explain that this is the assignment provided by the teacher and that this work will be collected at the end of class for a grade. If they have already completed this work, they should breeze through it as a review. There will always be resistance. The students rightly or wrongly assume that this is busy work and there will be no consequences if they do not do it. If you are not sure if it is busy work or not, tell them that it will be counted as classwork and not turning in the work will be counted as a zero. Let the teacher know in your notes who said what and who did or did not do their work. Put it in the notes, (see below). As I am walking the aisle, I try to engage the students and find out a little about them. You never know what's going to pop out. One time I asked a girl why she was just sitting there not working and she tells me that she is so angry at her father she wants to kill herself. After class, I called guidance and alerted them. They intervened. I don't know what type of intervention was provided but I saw her later in the day and she seemed better, less withdrawn and she said she was OK. I am constantly observing them for changes in behavior from the last time I had them in class. I note any changes in behavior/appearance to the teacher. As I walk around the classroom, I remind the students to write their names on their papers. As I cruise the aisles checking to see if they're working, I praise the students who are working by name. It also allows me to catch the names of the students who are not working. I will remind them to put their name on the paper and watch them do it. On the next lap, I will nudge them by name and they will ask how I knew their name. Too Funny.

Frequently they will follow-up with questions about me. This is an opening to a conversation. Sometimes I will not answer questions about my personal life, sometimes I will if I think it is in the best interest of the interaction. Some kids are just curious, some genuinely interested and some are looking for information to use to push my buttons. Be careful what information you provide and to whom. Also, be aware that generally anything you say will be communicated to the entire school via text or some other platform by the next class.

Students see the substitute teacher as an opportunity to not do work. They think what happens during that period stays forever in the time warp. (It's the kid version of "what happens in Las Vegas stays in Las Vegas".) At the beginning of the class, I tell the students that I take a lot of notes and record the good, the bad, and the ugly of the class period. During the class, I will ask the students who are doing their work their names if I don't know them and write them on my pad. When they ask why I tell them they are going on the good list. It's not uncommon for the other kids to all of the sudden want to know if and why they are not on the good list. This is an opening to explain that their behavior and decisions have not been up to standard. They will ask in what way and then deny that they are the culprit. That's okay. The fact that they were asking indicates they were listening to my response. Their immediate reaction is to deny responsibility but the seed has been planted. I have seen improved behavior in some students throughout a marking period as they try to get on the good list. There is also the bad list and I let the offenders know that the teacher will get a report.

Speaking of notes, I also give the teacher an overview of general class behavior, are they chatty, very chatty, out of control? Did they settle down quickly or did it take some nudging? If there is an incident that requires intervention, I give the teacher a detailed account of what happened. Depending on the severity, the teacher may have to write a report or a referral. A "referral" is an official report that goes to the administration. This will require detailed information so that the student's behavior can be addressed. By the way, the student will always deny their negative behavior and the other students may confirm the student's denial. It's good to have your account on paper so that if there are questions about what happened you have provided a record. Just provide the facts. Be careful not to let your emotions find their way into your report.

Some students also see the substitute teacher as someone to manipulate. No matter what the sub says, the students will tell you that it is not so. If the lesson plan involves reading something, they have already read it. If it involves worksheets, they have already done them. Mind you, the students who are saying this are generally the ones least likely to have done the work in the first place. Generally, the rest of the class will back what these students say. Also, there are usually one or two students in the class who will give you a believable answer if you ask them. (Many times, the teacher will tell you who the helpful students are in their notes to you.) If not, ask one of the other teachers in the hallway, who in this class will be helpful?

At some point you are going to encounter a student who will try the ultimate manipulation which is to call you a "racist". Some of these kids use racial pejoratives as part of their every day communication. Calling someone a racist to them is just another communication tool. Mind you, the student that pulls this nonsense is known for doing this type of thing. Do not get flustered. This is a teaching moment. In no case should you fall for this gambit or back off for fear of the student making an issue that you are a racist. To them this is the ultimate get out of jail free card. Also, do not get into an argument about whether you are a racist or not. Ask some questions, "why do you say that"? "What have I done to you that makes you say that?" Their response...." well you told me to be quiet and that person is talking and you haven't told them to be quiet." ??? That is their reason for calling me a racist. "Let's talk about why I have told you to be quiet at least 5 times. I can only deal with one individual at a time." I've had some worthwhile discussions with the class when someone said something like that. On one occasion after a short class discussion one girl turned to the other girl and said to her "what are you crazy?", the class laughed and we continued working. If the student requests to go to the office or some other administrator to complain that I am a racist I give them permission to go. But, I will call the dean/guidance counselor/administrator and let them know that so and so is coming down because they think I'm racist and they want to talk to about it. When you call their bluff, they will generally back off.

When a student asks to go someplace, (other teacher, media center, nurse, coach), I tell them that I will be contacting that person to see if it is OK for the student to go and make the call while the student is standing there. (See Keep a File) This eliminates a lot of requests.

If a student asks to go to the restroom and does not return in a timely manner, I call security or the Dean and report them as soon as I think that they have been gone too long. Also, if a student takes too long returning from somewhere, I confront them as to why it took so long. If they say they stopped to talk to another teacher, coach, or another person, I call that person to confirm that they saw the student. Once it gets around that you follow up like that, the students will be less likely to tell you they are going someplace and then go someplace else. If the student lied to me, they will get in trouble from three angles: their teacher, the person they said they were talking to, and me.

## 12 What If?

Every time I enter a school the main question on my mind is, **"What If"**! What if there is no lesson plan? What if a student falls down the steps between classes? What if I need assistance and the Deans are busy with more pressing matters? When I get into the classroom and look around, I am asking myself, "what if someone comes to the door that I don't know?" What if there's a fire? What if there is an active shooter? Is there a safe place for the students to go? What can I use as a weapon if necessary? What if the students tell me they have already completed the work the teacher left for them to do? (This happens all the time). What do I do if there are posters on the walls saying NO PHONES and the kids tell me, "Oh the teacher lets us listen to music"? Even though I have substituted at this school many times I am constantly looking for What Ifs? Substituting is a very fluid job and conditions and students change constantly. It's important to have thought about as many "What Ifs" as possible, and have a response plan in mind.

## 13 Keep a file

I keep a file with me at all times that has information that I may need during the day. This includes bell schedules for the various schools. Many classrooms post the bell schedules, some do not. Bell schedules differ according to grade or school. Schools also generally have multiple lunch periods which means that the periods for lunch "A" or lunch "B" are different. Students are not always truthful about when they are supposed to go to lunch and the clocks are not always synced to the bell system. It's helpful to have your own reference. I keep a school extension list for each school I sub at. There is nothing worse than needing to call someone and not being able to find the extension list in the classroom. The two minutes you waste looking for the extension list is a two-minute window that will provide chaos an opportunity to ensue.

## 14 **What Else to Bring**

Although most classrooms will have most of what you need at your disposal, every classroom is different. Looking for something I need and can't find disrupts the flow of the class, which is never a good thing. I keep a supply of pencils, pens, tissues, hall passes, detention slips, referral forms, and positive reinforcement tools that the school utilizes as well as other supplies I might need. Bring paper clips or binder clips. It's surprising how many classrooms I sub in where there are neither. When you are separating and organizing a classes work it needs to be bound somehow. Post-its aren't a bad idea to have either. I write fairly detailed notes about what happened in class. Sometimes there is lined paper available, sometimes the school has a form for that purpose. However, it usually doesn't provide enough space to adequately describe classroom activities. Bring a pad of lined paper. Again, there's probably paper someplace but I don't want to waste time looking for it. Hand sanitizer is not a bad idea. Yeah, it's a lot of stuff. It's your tool kit, like being a carpenter.

## 15 Classroom computers

Teachers incorporate computer usage into their lesson plans. It is a good tool for them. For substitute teachers not so much. If computer usage is in the lesson plan there is nothing you can do about it. Just beware of the pitfalls and try to hold the students' feet to the fire.

In middle school, there are several to 7 or 8 computers in every classroom. These are so the students can do individual study in math, reading, and language arts. Frequently the teacher will incorporate rotation of the students on the computers as part of their lesson plan. Generally, I find this to be troublesome for a couple of reasons. 1) If there are 7 computers in a classroom, at least one will not work, and you will not know that until the student has been fiddling with it for a while. Also, students know this and will sabotage the computer they are using and pretend they are trying to make it work. Every time a student logs in with Windows 10 the computer starts out going through an update routine that takes several minutes which gives the students a window to get into mischief. 2) The students will tell you that they are up to date on their computer minute requirements and will be playing games on the computer when confronted. Even after you remind them that the teacher will know whether they did their lessons or not and for how long, they will stick to their story. Computers are used as a great way to waste time.

Occasionally the teacher will move the class to the computer lab which is worse. Now there are 30 computers, 3 or 4 of which don't work. While the sub is trying to get one computer working there are 5 students goofing off. It's like playing Whack-a-Mole. This is not to take away from the fact that the schools have the personnel to oversee the computers and software. They cannot be everywhere all the time. They do their best and there are always a few students who will sabotage the computers.

# 16 **Communications**

As important as it is to communicate with the classroom teacher via notes, it is also very important to communicate with the other teachers on the team and administrative personnel. If there is an issue with a student, I will let one of the other teachers on the team know. They appreciate the feedback. They may have the student in a later period or have insight into the student's issues.

Whenever a student wants to go someplace, IE. nurse, Media Center, another teacher, etc. I will call that person for three reasons:

1)     To make sure the teacher/administrator is available and willing to see the student.
2)     To request that the teacher/administrator inform me if they have not arrived in a reasonable time, 5-7 minutes to let me know and I will call the Dean or security.
3)     To alert the students in the classroom that I am

checking up on them and if they are not where they are supposed to be there will be consequences. You will be surprised how many kids decide that they don't need to go after all when I start dialing the person's extension.

## 17 Maintaining Classroom Control

One of the primary responsibilities of a substitute teacher is to maintain discipline in the classroom. Every class has a dynamic based on the mix of the students. I have seen a student that is a problem in one class be manageable in another class. I'm not quite sure why. It could be the structure and clear boundaries that the classroom teacher has instilled or that the class has several positive kids with stronger personalities than the ones that normally act out. I don't know, I just know that the dynamic exists.

The majority of students are responsible, diligent students that don't require discipline. They may or may not like school but they understand that this is part of their growing up process and are resigned to making the best of it. Then there is the minority. These are the few who act out for any number of reasons, disrupting the classroom and distracting the majority of the class who just wants to do their work and move on.

A percentage of the responsible students will take their cue from the disruptive students if they observe that these kids can do what they want and without consequence. It's not difficult to identify the few that are going to take up most of your time. The difficult part is analyzing the best way to handle them without throwing the class into complete turmoil. Generally speaking, once the disruptive students have been identified the quicker their behavior is addressed the better the class will be. Coping with a disruptive student and not addressing or resolving the student's behavior will have an adverse effect on the other students' ability to do their work. Generally, the majority of the kids are as frustrated by their classmate's behavior as is the substitute. Also, the longer the disruptive student is "allowed" to act out the greater the chances that others see this as an opening to act out as well.

A substitute teacher has several tools at their disposal. These tools work to varying degrees. Sometimes a combination of tools is required. At the beginning of each class, I inform the kids that I take a lot of notes to keep the teacher apprised of what happened during the period. I tell them that I write down the good, the bad and the ugly. If there is a group of students that aren't really disruptive but they are not working I will go around the class with my pad and ask the students who are working what their names are, (If I don't know them) and write them down while telling them that I am letting the teacher know that they are doing their work quietly. I say this loud enough so those not working will know what I am doing and that I have not stopped by them. I also make a point of asking those that are not working what their name is, sometimes even if I know it. When they ask why I tell them that I am letting the teacher know that they are not working. I have some kids that will come up and ask which list they are on. This is an opening for a conversation; well what do you think, have you been working or not? Sometimes writing the names of the kids working and not working on the whiteboard is helpful. This can backfire in that the worst kids will see this as a badge and the fringe kids will act out to get their name on the board on the wrong side. You've got to know your audience on this one. The middle school I sub at has a positive reward system called "Cane Cash". Cane cash is given to students who have gone the extra mile whether it be helping the teacher, working diligently, or participating in class, etc. The Cane Cash can be spent in several ways on campus. I make a point of giving this to the students who are quietly working and being helpful. I want the students to know that I know who is working and who is not and that there are rewards for working and doing what you are supposed to do.

Every school has policies and procedures on how to deal with disruptive students. They range from a seat near the teacher to out of school suspension. You should know and understand the tools at your disposal at each school at which you substitute teach. Every school is different and besides, the norms differ from grade to grade and even classroom to classroom. Generally, I make the mistake of coping with the unruly students for too long during a period rather than dealing with them proactively early in the period. The consequence of this is that as the unruly student gets more confident as to how far he/she can push you and you ramp up your efforts to get him/her under control, the fringe students observing the unruly student will start testing you. Pretty soon instead of dealing with one or two unruly students, you have 5 or 6. As the period continues the students trying to do their work get frustrated because it is too loud and there are too many distractions. They will begin to talk among themselves rather than work. The bottom line is that you should be proactive in dealing with these kids. If they are in a group, make them sit by themselves preferably by the teacher's desk. If they continue, and the option is available, send them to another teacher's classroom. Most schools have unit leaders; teachers that have a lot more experience in dealing with disruptive kids than you. If push comes to shove and the student's behavior is out of your control; i.e., is not staying in their seat, is continuing to talk without permission, is being disrespectful toward you or acting aggressively, call the Dean/Security and have them removed. My experience is that most of the students want you to do something about a disruptive student. It is stressful to them hearing the teacher constantly talking/yelling at someone. If you wait too long the disruptive student will be able to rally some of the class to their defense and then you have lost control of the class. Even when you remove them the others will continue to talk, laugh among themselves and be distracting to the students who are trying to do their work. In conclusion, once you have made an effort to contain the potentially disruptive student and they have continued to act out, remove them. You will save the other students and you from angst. The rest of the class will generally get to work. The kids on the fringe have observed that you are serious about maintaining classroom decorum and will settle down.

Substituting at a high school is a different experience than working in a middle school. Generally, the students are smart enough to at least pretend that they are working. Classroom behavioral issues are far fewer. Although, if there is an issue it tends to be much more serious. In my experience, high-schoolers are known for two things:

1. Arriving to class late. Although there is a warning bell and then a final bell, high school kids cannot get to class on time. Even if it's across the hall from their last class. Log the time they arrive if they do not have a pass so the teacher knows. Make sure you mark them tardy on the attendance roster.
2. Leaving class with permission and not coming back in a timely fashion, or not coming back at all. If a student leaves class to go to the restroom, I check the time they leave and give them ten minutes. If they are not back I will ask the class how many miles it is to the restroom. Someone will answer that it's right down the hall. I will mention that the student has been gone too long and I am calling security. Several times a classmate has text-ed the kid and let them know I that I was calling security to report them missing. They got back pretty quickly. When I call security I talk loud enough for the class to hear what I am saying. If they get back before security finds them I take them into the hall for a conversation about why their behavior is unacceptable. Then I will call security while they are standing with me and explain that the student is back and ask, "What should I do with them?". I then write a note to the teacher letting them know that the student

was a distraction to the class and why. Frequently the student will return and tell me they were talking to another teacher, adviser or coach. I will call the person they say they were with to verify they are telling the truth. Sometimes when I start dialing the kid will confess that they were not with that person. That's another strike. I will continue calling the teacher and let them know that the student used their name to lie to me. Occasionally they are telling the truth. Then we have a conversation about being inconsiderate to the other students that need to go to the restroom and can't because that student had the restroom pass. As it gets around the school that you follow up and check on their stories many of them will think twice before pulling that game again.

## 18 End of Period/Block

The most precarious part of each period is the ten minutes at the end of the class. The students start to get edgy about ten minutes before the bell. They lose focus and start talking and goofing around. At the same time, the sub is losing focus and thinking about the next class. This is a bad dynamic and is a situation where bad things can happen. Frequently this is where two "best friends" will start goofing around pushing and shoving each other or taking something that belongs to the other. This quickly escalates into one of them getting angry and striking out, or an innocent bystander getting involved by accident. **Do Not Let This Happen!** When you intervene, they will always say "we're just fooling around", "we're best friends", they might be but only bad things can happen when they are fooling around and not paying attention and YOU are not paying attention. Never let down your guard in the last ten minutes. Ideally, don't let them out of their seats until the bell rings. Under no circumstances should they open the door before the bell rings. I had a student last year in middle school who had been driving me crazy all period. At the end of class, he pushed to the front of the line and opened the door. He was either pushed out into the hallway or went out on his own. I yelled at him to get back in the classroom. As he was coming in the bell rang and the kids stormed out. Somehow, he got his finger caught in the closing door. These things are heavy. He started shrieking. Not realizing what happened, I'm yelled at him to get out. The teacher across the hall heard the commotion and ran over to my classroom. He must have thought I was beating him. He determined what happened, determined that there are probably no broken bones and sent him to the nurse. This should not have happened if I were paying attention at the end of class. I learned a good lesson that day, unfortunately at the expense of a 12-year-old. Thankfully he was not hurt.

## 19 Fighting

At some point during your stint/career as a substitute teacher, a fight will break out somewhere in your presence. This topic was briefly covered in our substitute orientation class. The bottom line was that a teacher has no legal responsibility to intervene besides calling the school resource authorities. They did touch on the difference between girl's fights and boy's fights. And OMG is there a difference. Boys will generally disengage as soon as an authority figure intervenes. Girls will fight until they are too tired to stand, they will take a break and go back at it. Generally, there is a lot of hair-pulling. As the keeper of peace in the classroom, it is not reasonable to stand back and wait for other authorities to get to the classroom. You are between a rock and a hard place. You shouldn't be touching the kids yet you can't risk someone getting hurt. If possible, get between the parties, talking firmly, not yelling while telling them to calm down. If possible, extend your arms and place them between the two parties with palms facing each other and move your arms apart separating the combatants. This surprisingly works. I've done this with boys fighting. They separated and ran, that's another issue. Girls are more difficult and you have to be very careful how and where you touch them. You have to do what you have to do to prevent someone from getting hurt. You may have to pick one up and move her out of range, mind you there could very well be ramifications to doing this. Also, the whole hair-pulling thing is problematic. I'm not sure they can unlock their fists from the other girl's hair when they are in this state.

Your best bet is to prevent the fight before it gets to physical conflict. This is where the substitute has to be ever vigilant and be observing what's going on in the classroom at all times. Generally, fights happen in stages. One person doesn't just walk up and wallop someone. There is a lead up to the main event. Either one or both students will be mocking, harassing, poking or yelling at one another. **Don't let this escalate.** Intervene by telling them to knock it off and position yourself between them. With guys, they will tell you that they are "just messing around and are best friends". This may be the case but that's no excuse. Tell them to Cool it or you will hit the call button. It's best to move their seats for the period just in case. Girls will tell you, "No, no it's OK, we're just messing around" **No, it's not OK**. Again, separate them. The next boy or girl that says something to the other should be removed from the class. If not, this will escalate. This is where the substitute has to be ever vigilant and observing what's going on in the classroom at all times. My experience is that fights are most likely to happen in the last ten minutes of the class. If they are allowed to migrate to the door before the bell you are asking for trouble. There is always pushing, shoving, and goofing around and all the kids are clumped together. It's a perfect storm for someone to do something that upsets someone else either intentionally or by accident. The other scenario is at the beginning of class when the kids are filing in. Generally, the teacher is standing at the doorway watching the hallway activity and keeping an eye on the kids in the classroom. As soon as you sense, hear or see a couple of kids starting to rough house, nip it in the bud. This all sounds like so much common sense until you're in the middle of a melee. The bottom line is vigilance. Remember, there is also the dynamic that once the kids realize there is a substitute teacher, they have already let their self control and focus down. The behavioral expectations that the classroom teacher imposes are out the window

## 20 Phones

Use of phones in class is a big problem. The kids are forever texting, chatting, taking pictures, watching movies and receiving phone calls...... sometimes from parents, during class. (This blows my mind).

Policies vary. Recently there is a trend toward no phones at all. The classrooms have posters all over the place indicating no phones. Some teachers require the phones to be placed in a container when they enter class. Some require them to be turned off and put in their backpack. Some teachers allow the use of phones for research or to listen to music when working independently.

Generally, I try to follow the teacher's lead. If I'm not sure what the teacher's policy is I will ask a neighboring teacher for guidance. Sometimes my decision on the use of phones in the classroom is determined by the tenor of student behavior. If the class seems to be engaged in work and there is a request to listen to music, I will give permission. Sometimes this will be blanket permission and sometimes just to the individual asking. If I give one student permission but not another, this can cause a problem, which I fully expect and treat it as a teaching moment. I always have a good reason to deny somcone the use of their phone while allowing another student to use their phone. This provides an opportunity to discuss that there are rewards and consequences for behavior. The offending student will never say, "yeah you're right, sorry about that", but hopefully at some level, they get the message.

There is always the caveat that I will change my mind either individually or class-wide if I observe that students are tending to be less engaged or if I observe that they are watching something or playing a game. On occasion, I will take a student's phone if they are abusing the privilege. They will tell me I can't do that. I don't get into a discussion of whether I can or can't. If they want to make an issue out of it and report me for some reason that's okay. I've never had anyone follow through or at least it has not been brought to my attention. If it gets to the point where I attempt to take the phone and they refuse, they have to be removed. No questions or discussion.

## 21 Teacher's Helpers

Many times, there are students who are assigned to a class as a "teacher's helper". I incorrectly assumed these were students who are considered responsible. Wrong assumption. There isn't a criterion that the student has to meet to be a teacher's helper. Some teacher's helpers are responsible and will help you pass out papers, grade assignments, run errands, and generally do anything you ask. There are others who are not helpful or responsible. They might be one of the more disruptive kids in the class. They should be treated as any other student. If they misbehave, they must be dealt with. The sooner the better.

## 22 Substitute Teachers Legal Responsibilities

While doing some research on the laws governing teachers/substitute teachers legal responsibilities I found a great article written by John M. Drye, Esq., **Educational Resources: Tort Liability101: When are Teachers Liable?** This is information that I have not been exposed to in any training. Please see the link to the article. **Worth reading:**

www.educator-resources.com/pdf/Teacher Tort Liability.pdf

## 23 **Personal Attention**

Kids thrive on personal attention, positive and negative. I try to provide positive personal attention whenever possible. Otherwise, some good kids may act out to get attention. Calling them by name is huge. I have to make an effort to remember the names of the students that do what they are supposed to do without fanfare. It's difficult because as a sub I may not have reason to call them very often. When I do get the opportunity, I want to call them by name. Their faces light up! I get to know the names of the kids that act out pretty quickly for obvious reasons.

Some kids like personal attention whether it be a hug, a fist bump, a high five, or a handshake. Per training, if you hug a student it should be from the side, not the front. Some teachers hug. I don't hug. This has led to several situations where the kid's feelings were hurt because they took my reaction as a personal rejection and were embarrassed. I had to explain that I don't hug anyone because I don't feel comfortable doing that. I will do the handshake, high five, fist pump stuff if it is under the proper circumstances. This past week I substitute taught at a high school. This kid came in 15 minutes late with no pass and wanted to shake my hand. I think this was an attempt to get me to acknowledge that his behavior was acceptable. I declined and told him to sit down, he was late and I was marking him as tardy. He got upset and made a point of telling the other students that I would not shake his hand simply because he was late. He went on for a few seconds then sat down and pouted. Later as I trolled the room checking to see who was working, (as opposed to playing Fortnight), I noticed that he was quietly working. He worked all period quietly. At the end of class as the kids were getting ready to bolt, I came to him, acknowledged his work and stuck out my hand which he accepted with a smile. He was so flustered he left his phone on his desk and had to come back several minutes later to get it and thanked me.

## 24 Making Mistakes

Please understand substitute teaching is a very fluid situation. No matter how prepared you think you are there will always be a situation that you did not account for. The purpose of this pamphlet is to help raise your awareness to help you minimize those situations. But be cognizant of the fact that when you are dealing with these situations you will make mistakes. Maybe you will say the wrong thing to someone. Maybe you will wrongly accuse someone of something. Maybe you will inadvertently embarrass a student. Some mistakes only you will know about, others the kids will know about, and others everybody will know about. Some will be inconsequential and others may have a consequence. If I am wrong and I know that I am wrong, I apologize to the student. Depending on the situation either in front of the class or privately as they are leaving class. This actually can go a long way toward the students respecting you and viewing you a little differently. Not as someone who likes to throw their weight around but someone willing to step up and admit their error. Granted, admitting something can come back and bite you but I believe that doing the right thing usually defuses a situation.

If you are overly concerned about doing the wrong thing you will not be effective. Plan the best you can and use your common sense. Always keep the best interest of the class and students front and center. Document everything, the sooner the better. Whether a mistake is a big one or a little one depends in large part on parties you have no control over, i.e. students, administrators, and parents. Also, keep perspective, something you did that you think is egregious may not even register with the kids. Having your side of the story documented before a question arises can go a long way to defusing a situation. Whom should the documentation go to? Generally, to the teacher. Let them know what happened and your response, even if you are not comfortable with your response. The teacher knows the kids and maybe the families. If a question comes up after you're gone and the teacher is aware of your side, they can respond before a situation gets out of control. If you think it's necessary, let the Dean of Students or Vice-Principal know. Generally, when a situation gets to this point the administration is already involved anyway.

## 25 IEP (Individualized Educational Plans) and 504 Plans

**IEP**- Short for Individualized Education Program requires that a student have one or more of the thirteen disabilities listed in the Individuals with Disabilities Education Act (IDEA).[1] A plan details the support and special educational services (such as speech therapy or multisensory reading instruction) a school will provide to meet the individual needs of a student with a disability who qualifies for special education. [2]

**504 Plan**- Is a section in the civil rights law, Section 504 of the Rehabilitation Act of 1973. The scope of section 504 is broader that the scope of the IDEA. Therefore a student may be eligible for a 504 plan that is not eligible for an IEP and in a special education program. It is a plan that lists the accommodations a school will provide, such as audiobooks, note-taking aids or extended time to complete tests, so that a student with a disability, who may or may not be in the special educational program, has equal access to the general education curriculum.[3]

As I touched on above, in the Pre class preparation section these plans may be provided in the substitute folder. If so they are helpful. If not be aware that every class you sub in will have several students with some kind of support plan. This information is useful in context to help you make decisions during class regarding the performance or nonperformance of a student. **This information is not to be discussed in open class even if the student brings it up.**

I have found that generally other class members are aware of another student's issues/plan and will help you if something arises. Once I had a student come up to me and tell me he had to go to the nurse at 1:30 to get medication for his diabetes. Before I could even call the nurse to confirm another student let me know that in fact, that was the case, he goes every day. Good to know. Based upon what I knew about both students I felt comfortable that this was true.

Be especially careful when dealing with students who are not doing anything in class. This kid may have an IEP that you don't know about and there is something you should be doing that you don't know about, i.e. providing auditory cues, working with them individually, working with another student, working independently on the computer, etc. Before you reprimand them for not working ask probing questions. Again, many times other students will guide you. The student you are asking may not be forthcoming but his/her classmates might be. Some students don't want the fact that they have been classified to be recognized. They will do the best they can without asking for help. Some students use it as a weapon to get out of doing work. I had one student tell me that he did not have to do the work the teacher assigned because it was too hard and his IEP said that if he thought the work was too hard he didn't have to do it. I asked him if he had even tried and he told me

NO. The conversation continued without any progress. I later asked the teacher about this kid and was told: " oh yeah, and his mother supports him, and... she's a teacher at the school." Then there was the student who told me that their IEP addressed a specific issue I questioned them about. During lunch, I went to the person responsible for the IEP plans and was told that that student had never been evaluated. She was not in the system. Nice Try!

1 HG.ORG. "HGEXPERTS.COM." EXPERT WITNESS DIRECTORY,
HTTPS://WWW.HGEXPERTS.COM/EXPERT-WITNESS-ARTICLES/WHICH-IS-BEST-FOR-MY-HANDICAPPED-CHILD-S-EDUCATION-A-504-PLAN-OR-AN-IEP-43398.

2, 3 TEAM, UNDERSTOOD. "EXPERTS WEIGH IN: 'CAN MY CHILD CHANGE TEACHERS MID-YEAR?"." CAN YOUR CHILD CHANGE TEACHERS MID-YEAR? | ADVICE ON CHANGING TEACHERS, UNDERSTOOD, 5 AUG. 2019,
HTTPS://WWW.UNDERSTOOD.ORG/EN/SCHOOL-LEARNING/PARTNERING-WITH-CHILDS-

SCHOOL/TEACHER-RELATED-ISSUES/EXPERTS-
WEIGH-IN-CAN-MY-CHILD-CHANGE-TEACHERS-
MID-YEAR.

## 26 Conclusions

Being a substitute teacher is not an easy undertaking. You are in a very fluid situation. You are required to make many decisions very quickly with the very limited information that will impact young people with which you have little or no experience, possibly in a school that you have not previously been in. Your best tools are preparation, common sense and an accepting attitude.

Understand that the nature of some kids is that they are going to try and push your buttons and manipulate you. If this is a problem then maybe you should think twice about being a substitute teacher. The majority of the students you will meet are great kids who want to do the work that has been assigned and move on. Also, understand that the majority of the class is just as fed up with the antics of a few as you are. Dealing with the minority as quickly as possible is key to maintaining an orderly classroom environment where the majority of the kids can concentrate on doing their lessons.

Preparation is key. Bring your toolkit with all of the things that you may need during the day. Looking for a hall pass or extension list is a distraction that is not necessary. Upon entering a new school or even a school you have been in before keep your eyes and ears open for any information that may be helpful or that has changed, ie. schedule changes, school events, policy changes since the last time you were there.

When you arrive at the classroom take a minute or two to just observe the setup of the room. How are the desks arranged? Look for information on the whiteboard, posters on the wall. Generally, you can get a sense of the teacher's mindset and how they conduct their classes by observing the classroom setup. If there is a projector or sound system that will be used for announcements or during the lesson figure out how to use it before class starts. If the lesson plan involves using computers in the classroom, turn them on, see which ones work.

Common sense is key. Keep it simple. Do not over complicate a situation by over-thinking it. Use the information you have, get as much additional information as you can, make a plan and put it into action. The making of the plan and putting it to action may take a minute. That's all the time you will have. Document, document, document. Leave the teacher a lot of notes. Don't be wordy, just the facts. Give the teacher names of students that did what they were supposed to do and those that did not. They need specifics. "Some kids acted out" is not helpful. Who?

What did you do in response?

Check your baggage at the door. You have no idea where these kids are coming from or what their home lives are like. They may dress differently; their hair will be different than you may be used to. Their way of addressing you and communicating with you may be different than you are used to or that you are expecting. Do not prejudge them. Keep your mind open and your attitude and emotions in check. Your job is to maintain the continuity and consistency of the teacher's lesson plan and maintain classroom order. You know upfront that a minority of the kids will try to push your buttons. Don't let that happen. Be professional, accepting, honest and firm. Good Luck.

# 27 Misc. Information

1. Xfacto wall mounted pencil sharpeners are not a good value. Rarely do I see one that works.
2. 6th graders have thimble size bladders and will be constantly asking to go to the restroom.
3. Don't be shocked when a girl tells you she has to "pee".
4. Girls will ask to go to the restroom because of girl issues/problems. I do not refuse them permission. Even if they have been to the restroom that period.
5. DO NOT USE THE STUDENTS BATHROOMS! I know that's common sense but...

# ABOUT THE AUTHOR

I am retired living in the beautiful state of Florida. Before spending 31 years in the audiovisual business, I was a Probation Officer in NJ for eight years. My BS degree is in Criminal Justice/Correction from Youngstown State University with an AAS in Police Science.

My wife, Rose, and I have been married for 44 years and reside in Port St. Lucie Florida. We have three grown kids. My interests are tennis, reading, going to the beach and working out.

I began substitute teaching at a charter school in Broward Cty., Florida about three years ago. Upon moving to St. Lucie Cty., I applied and was hired as a substitute teacher at a local charter school. Little did I know, having no experience as a teacher that I would be the permanent/temporary 7th-grade Physical Science teacher. My tenure as a teacher was supposed to be for a couple of weeks but lasted for the first marking period. Talk about baptism under fire. I am currently a substitute teacher at that charter school for grades 6-12. I am also a substitute teacher in the county school system at a middle school and high school. Being a substitute teacher observing the kids as they grow and mature from year to year is very rewarding.